This book should be returned to any branch of the
Lancashire County Library on or before the date shown

KENNETH WAISSMAN & MAXINE FOX
in association with **ANTHONY D'AMOTO**
present

GREASE
A New 50's Rock 'N Roll Musical

Book, Music & Lyrics by
JIM JACOBS & WARREN CASEY

*Musical Supervision and
Orchestrations by*
MICHAEL LEONARD

*Musical Direction
Vocal and Dance Arrangements by*
LOUIS ST. LOUIS

Scenery by
DOUGLAS W. SCHMIDT

Costumes by
CARRIE F. ROBBINS

Lighting by
KARL EIGSTI

Sound by
JACK SHEARING

Hairstyles Created by
JIM SULLIVAN

General Management
THEATRE NOW, Inc.

Press Representation
**BETTY LEE HUNT
ASSOCIATES**

Production Stage Manager
JOE CALVAN

Musical Numbers and Dances Staged by
PATRICIA BIRCH

Directed by
TOM MOORE

Piano Reduction by Ronnie Ball

A publication of
EDWIN H. MORRIS & COMPANY
A Division of MPL Communications, Inc.

PREMIERE PERFORMANCE AT THE EDEN THEATRE, N.Y.C.
February 14, 1972

CAST
(In Order of Appearance)

MISS LYNCH . . . . Dorothy Leon
PATTY SIMCOX . . . . Ilene Kristen
EUGENE FLORCZYK . . . . Tom Harris
JAN . . . . Garn Stephens
MARTY . . . . Katie Hanley
BETTY RIZZO . . . . Adrienne Barbeau
DOODY . . . . James Canning
ROGER . . . . Walter Bobbie
KENICKIE . . . . Timothy Meyers
SONNY LA TIERRI . . . . Jim Borrelli
FRENCHY . . . . Marya Small
SANDY DUMBROWSKI . . . . Carole Demas
DANNY ZUKO . . . . Barry Bostwick
VINCE FONTAINE . . . . Don Billett
JOHNNY CASINO . . . . Alan Paul
CHA-CHA DI GREGORIO . . . . Kathi Moss
TEEN ANGEL . . . . Alan Paul

SCENES

Act I

Scene 1: Reunion
Scene 2: Cafeteria and School Steps
Scene 3: Pajama Party
Scene 4: Street Corner
Scene 5: Schoolyard
Scene 6: Park

Act II

Scene 1: Kids' Homes
         School Gym
Scene 2: Front of Burger Palace
Scene 3: Drive-In Movie
Scene 4: Jan's Party
Scene 5: Inside Burger Palace

ORCHESTRA INSTRUMENTATION

2 Reeds
2 Guitars
Drums
Bass
Piano Conductor Score

MUSICAL NUMBERS

No. 1

RYDELL ALMA MATER
Act I

By
WARREN CASEY
JIM JACOBS

Moderate 4 *(High school assembly style)*

ENSEMBLE:

As I go trav-'ling down life's high-way, what-ev-er course my for-tunes may fore-tell, I shall not go a-lone on my way, for thou shalt al-ways be with me, Ry - dell. When I seek

8

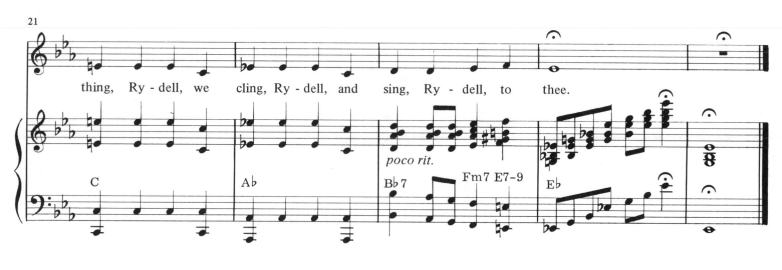

thing, Ry - dell, we cling, Ry - dell, and sing, Ry - dell, to thee.

C   Ab   Bb7   Fm7   E7-9   Eb

poco rit.

Cue: MISS LYNCH: Research and marketing

Moderately *(lightly)*

Cue: I was only joking.

Grandioso

C   Ab   Bb   Cm6/D   D7

poco rit.

8va bassa - - - - -

Segue No. 2

No. 2

RYDELL ALMA MATER PARODY

Cue: EUGENE: Just the way we always remember them!

Moderately bright 4 (♩ = 160)

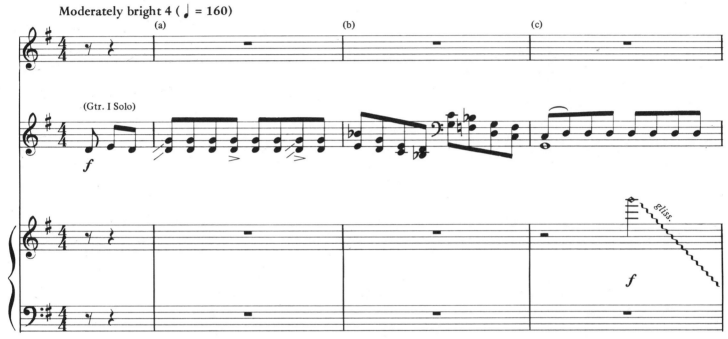

I saw a dead skunk on the high-way and I was

ENSEMBLE:

D., Ry - dell? Could be, Ry - dell, _ you ought to see the fac - ul -

ty.

If Mis - ter Clean, Ry - dell, has

seen Ry - dell, he'd just turn green and dis - ap - pear.

I'm out - ta

A7   F#7   B7

luck, Ry - dell, dead duck, Ry - dell. I'm stuck, Ry - dell, right here.

E   C   D   G

Vamp till lights up on girls

(Gtr. Solo) (ad lib)

(R.H. Electric Piano)

(L.H. Acoustic Piano)

No. 3

SUMMER NIGHTS

22

60

just turned eigh-teen._____ DANNY: She was good,

uh - huh, uh - huh.

shu - da bop - bop, yeah._____

B♭   C7   F7   B♭

62

know what I mean._ BOTH: Sum-mer heat, boy and girl meet,_ then _

F7   B♭7   E♭   A♭   B♭   C7

No. 3a

SCENE CHANGE NO. 2

Cue: School bell

Moderately bright 4 (♩ = 160)
(If electric piano, play R.H. only. If acoustic piano, play R.H. and L.H.)

No. 4   # THOSE MAGIC CHANGES

Cue: Terrific! You wanna hear it again?

24
turn to me, don't go a - way a - gain, oh, make them
3
La la la la.
G7
C
26
play a - gain the mu - sic I wan - na hear as once a -
Am
F
28
gain you whis - per in my ear.
BOYS and GIRLS:
C
A
G7
C
Am

No. 4a

SCENE CHANGE NO. 3

Cue: MR. LATTIERI: Aren't you due right now in detention hall?

(If electric piano, play R.H. on electric piano, L.H. on acoustic piano. If no electric piano, play fuller voicings)

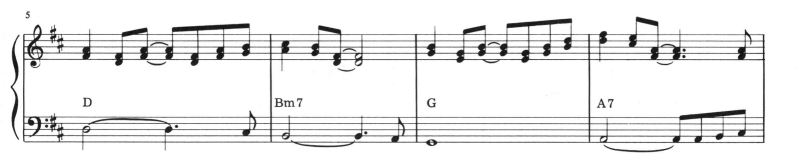

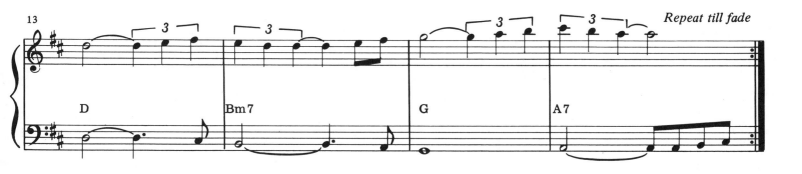

No. 5

FREDDY, MY LOVE

Cue: Hey, what do you say to a guy in a letter, anyway?

No. 5a

CROSSOVER TO GREASED LIGHTNING

Cue: Rizzo leaves through window

Segue No. 6

No. 6

GREASED LIGHTNING

Cue: DANNY: The one and only Greased Lightnin'

Drums fill: (Catches all vocal entrances)

No. 6a RIZZO'S ENTRANCE AND CHASER

Cue: RIZZO: Good Humor truck

When Sandy reaches center of platform, orchestra is cut! Drums play march cadence (snare and bass drum). Sandy does cheer, then does a fall (split) caught on a cymbal crash.

No. 7

RYDELL'S FIGHT SONG

Cue: SANDY: C'mon, let's practice

glo - ry of Ry - dell ev - er - more.

(Fade on lights up)

No. 8

MOONING

Warning Cue: ROGER: Wish you'da been there too.
Cue: JAN: You do?

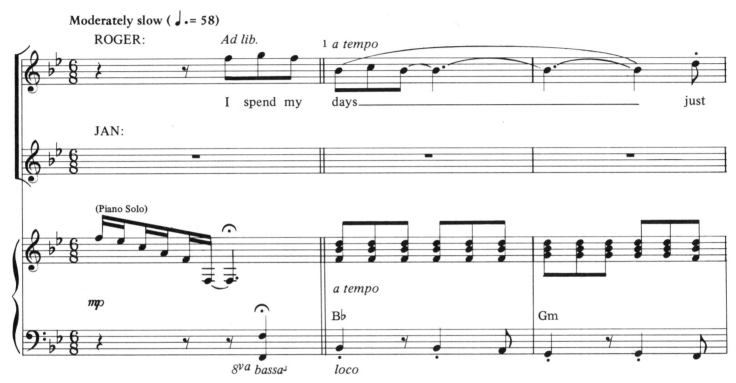

LOOK AT ME, I'M SANDRA DEE

No. 9

Cue: RIZZO: Right you guys

filth - y paws off my silk - y drawers, would you pull that

stuff with An - nette? As for you, Troy

Don - a - hue, I know what you wan - na

No. 10

WE GO TOGETHER

Cue: DANNY: You wanna be chaperone

waaah.__

When we go out at night,__ and stars are

shin - ing bright__ up in the skies a - bove.__

T. Sax. 1 (corny)

Or at the high school dance,__ where you can

No. 11 SHAKIN' AT THE HIGH SCHOOL HOP
Act II

IT'S RAINING ON PROM NIGHT

Cue: VINCE FONTAINE: It's raining on Prom night

Segue No. 12A

No. 12a

SCENE CHANGE
INTO HIGH SCHOOL HOP

No. 12b UNDERSCORE—HIGH SCHOOL HOP

Cue: VINCE FONTAINE: If you got a steady get her ready

Repeat only if necessary

MARTY: I had a hickey on my neck

87

90

ROGER: Are you crippled?

93

D

97 A little faster — Beguine (♩ = 126)

No. 12c

ENTER MISS LYNCH

Cue: JOHNNY CASINO: Our very own Miss Lynch

No. 12d

ENTER VINCE FONTAINE

Cue: MISS LYNCH: Vince Fontaine – Mister Fontaine!

(THE GILLETTE FIGHT SONG)

No. 13

BORN TO HAND JIVE

Cue: VINCE FONTAINE: And away we go!

ba - by.___ Born to hand jive, ba - by.___

(Acoustic Piano)

(Dance)
(Tenor Sax I Solo)

No. 13a

CROSSOVER—LAST DANCE—
OUT OF HIGH SCHOOL HOP

Cue: VINCE FONTAINE: Last dance - ladies choice

No. 14

BEAUTY SCHOOL DROPOUT

Warning Cue: FRENCHY: Wouldn't that be neat
Cue: Somebody always there

Segue No. 14A

No. 14a BEAUTY SCHOOL DROPOUT—REPRISE

Cue: Frenchy throws diploma

Moderate 2 (♩. = 72)
TEEN ANGEL:

Ba - by, you blew it! ____ You put our

good ad - vice to shame. ____ How could you do it? ____

Bet - cha Dear Ab - by'd say the same. ____ Guess there's

No. 14b SCENE CHANGE INTO ALONE AT THE DRIVE-IN MOVIE

Cue: ROGER: Oh, shit!

No. 15

ALONE AT THE DRIVE-IN MOVIE

Tape Cue: Wolf howl

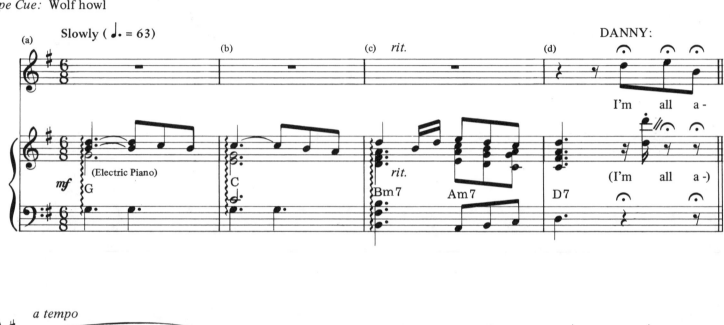

No. 16

ROCK AND ROLL PARTY QUEEN

No. 17 THERE ARE WORSE THINGS I COULD DO

Cue: RIZZO: You just listen to me, Miss Sandra Dee

Direct Segue No. 18

No. 18

LOOK AT ME I'M SANDRA DEE—REPRISE

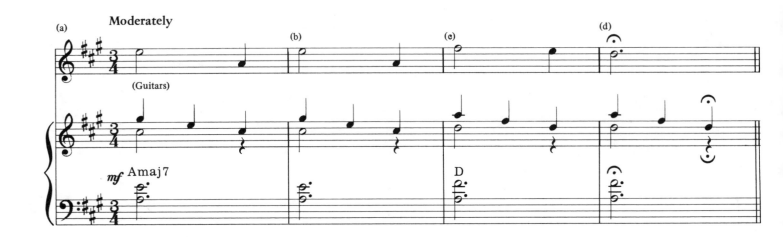

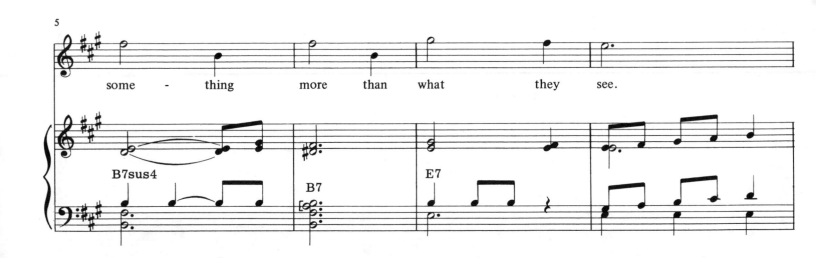

Direct Segue No. 18A

No. 18a SCENE CHANGE OUT OF LOOK AT ME I'M SANDRA DEE—REPRISE

No. 19

ALL CHOKED UP

I'll for - give___ what you put me thru,___ 'cause I

do be - lieve___ you real - ly love me too.___ I look in your eyes,___ the

suf - fer - ing dies,___ uh huh, I'm all choked up.___

* Top voice sounds 8ve lower.

Hey, hey, hey, hey, I'm all choked up.

Hey, hey, hey, hey, I'm all choked up.

B7+9

E7

F#7

8va bassa -

B

E7

F#7

B   E/B   B   E/B

8va -

loco

B   E/B   B   E/B   B   E/B   B   E/B   B

gliss.

Direct Segue No. 19A

No. 19a CROSSOVER

Segue No. 20

No. 20

FINALE

Cue: SANDY: Yeah, I'm all choked up

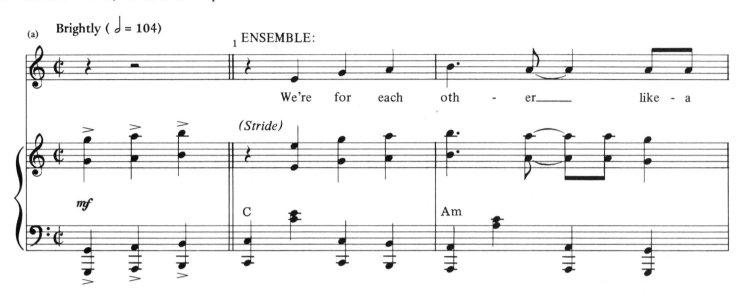

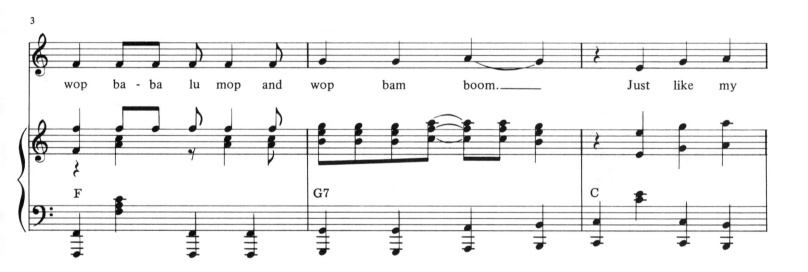

179

No. 21

BOWS AND EXIT MUSIC

No. 22

HOUSE EXIT MUSIC

Twice Through — Then Jam – Then Out